How To Build An EXCELLENT CHILD

An Easy Guide to

Effortless, Subliminal Parenting

by Expert Talent Developer

Meredith M. Day

Copyright © 2021 Meredith M Day

All rights reserved.

ISBN: 9781647042899

DEDICATION

To my wonderful son Robert,
my Mother, Father and Great Aunt,
as well as all the parents who truly
want to be the very best parent they can be.

Free Lullaby Music included with purchase!

Email proof of purchase to:

Meredith.M.Day@gmail.com

CONTENTS

	Acknowledgments	i
1	If You Are Too Busy To Read A Book	1
2	What is A Subliminal Parent	3
3	What Is Subliminal Parenting	5
4	Will I Make A Good Parent	7
5	In The Womb	11
6	Listen To Your Fetus	15
7	Rest And Cravings	17
8	What Baby Weight	19
9	Decorating Baby's Room	21
10	Nursing And Baby Bottles	23
11	Teething	25
12	Is My Child Sick	27
13	Your Child's First Shot	29
14	What's The Big Deal About Water	31
15	Is This Really Colic	37
16	Assessing Your Child's Cries	39
17	Crib Death	41
18	The Family Bed	43
19	The Terrible 2s	47
20	Choosing Child Care	49

THE SUBLIMINAL PARENT

21	What's The Deal About Diapers	55
22	Effortless Toilet Training	57
23	Enforcing no	61
24	How to Manage A Tantrum	65
25	Why Your Child Won't Eat	67
26	About Bullys and Bullying	73
27	A Parent's Responsibility	75
28	Packing your Child's Lunch	77
29	What Is School For	79
30	Homework Practices	81
31	When Should Your Child Have a Pet	83
32	Parenting A Special Child	85
33	The Child Actor	87
34	Building An Excellent Child	91
35	Parent's Puberty Survival Guide	95
36	Your Child's Brain	101
37	How to Fight Childhood Obesity	103
38	Last, But Not Least	105
	About The Author	107

THE SUBLIMINAL PARENT

ACKNOWLEDGMENTS

I wrote this edition in the middle of the 2020 pandemic.

A daunting, scary time for parents.

A time to pray for all the good people,
everywhere.

1 IF YOU ARE TOO BUSY TO READ A BOOK

If you are overwhelmed and too busy to read a book, remember this above all:

Your Child Will Become Whatever You Tell Them They Are.

Your child will treat you with the same love, attention and respect that you show them.

Best Wishes

Meredith M Day

THE SUBLIMINAL PARENT

2 WHAT IS A SUBLIMINAL PARENT

This is the Best Parenting Operations Manual you can read!

The Subliminal Parent is effortless if you do it right. If you don't, good parenting can be very challenging.

In this operations manual are easy to follow, simple parenting techniques. If used as directed, you will have easy remedies for the typical challenges of parenthood.

I had my child at 37. Prior to that I was able to watch all my friends raise their children. I saw what worked and what didn't work. I put all that knowledge to work with my own child. I edited out what didn't work and kept what did work.

Over the years I have also managed and developed many talented young children for the entertainment industry, including children on a variety of spectrums. Even an autistic girl I managed has become a talented, very successful singer and voice over artist.

I am going to pass this valuable experience on to you in the following operations manual.

My body of experience has allowed me to develop methods that deliver excellent results. If they are done right, they are effortless! You will be able to be an excellent, **Subliminal Parent** even when exhausted and distracted!

Unfortunately, one doesn't find out if they've been a good parent until their children are grown. Too late for a do over.

You need to rely on advice from people you trust. Things that may seem to make sense at the time, in the long run may make no sense at all. I have created this book to help you avoid all those dangerous pitfalls. Avoid misinformation from very well-meaning friends and relatives.

I am going to show you how to be an excellent parent by parenting *Subliminally*.

Subliminal Parenting is effortless and fun. The excellent parent is a TRUE subliminal parent. Be prepared to become an excellent **Subliminal Parent**!

Subliminal Parenting is the most valuable gift you can give your child, and the EASIEST way to be an excellent parent.

The best news of all is that your child will train their children the way you did if their growth experience was pleasant and nurturing.

Welcome aboard!

3 WHAT IS SUBLIMINAL PARENTING

In the following chapters I am going to show you how to train subliminally.

Parents commonly train by instruction and punishment, correction. Excellent parents train subliminally. Subliminal Parenting is the method of teaching your child without seeming to do so.

Subliminal Parenting is based on the proven truth that children will copy everything their parent does and says. You are their subliminal teacher. Before words have meaning, your actions and expressions teach your child.

If the parent allows their child to participate and the parent does what they want the child to do, the child will imitate that behavior. Likewise, the child will reflect the opinions and morals of the parents.

You need to decide who you want your child to be, and you need to be that. Show them that side of you.

If there is something you do not want to pass on to your child, do not do that. It is that simple.

With true Subliminal Parenting, the parent does not even have to disturb their focus in order to interact with their child. Instead the parent gives of themselves, allows their child to participate, thereby building an excellent child.

4 WILL I MAKE A GOOD PARENT

When planning a family, it is common to wonder if you will make a good parent. The first thing to consider is your lifestyle.

Many of the best parents comment that before they had their own children, they were intolerant of other people's children. They were afraid that when their own children came along, they would be just as intolerant.

The truth is that a parent bonds with their own child, and those individuals who were intolerant of other people's children, in many cases prove to be more attentive to their own children's needs than those who could ignore their friend's children.

The most important thing to consider is how much of your time you are willing to give to your prospective family. Is your child going to be raised by a nanny or outside caregivers?

Will you personally enjoy the cleaning, cooking, nursing, teaching and defending you will be doing, or would you prefer to lose yourself in an all-consuming, lucrative, high powered career?

Being able to have both a high-powered career and raise a family is very possible, doing it well is extremely demanding. You will need a spouse or a caregiver, man or woman, who is able to stay home with your children. Another alternative are the corporations, such as Steven Spielberg's film company, Amblin, that make provisions for the parents to bring their children to work.

If your spouse also has a high-powered career, then most likely others will raise your children the majority of the time.

Your children will acquire the knowledge and morals of the outside caregiver, and in the long run will probably bond most heavily to the individuals that spend the most waking time with. This, in such cases, may not be you or your working spouse.

They will, of course, acknowledge you as their parent, but they will truly love their fulltime caregiver. This is a real danger because in many cases the parent will arbitrarily change caregivers from time to time. Changing without considering the psychological damage to the child resulting from the abrupt separation from someone the child loves.

These children quickly learn not to give their love, that will affect their relationship with the biological parents as well. It will also affect their personal relationships ongoing.

You will have to decide if having a family at this time in your life is so important that you can justify others raising your children. You might decide to wait until you can devote focused time and attention to your children.

Older parent's children tend to do better in school due to the fact that it is not a high priority to go out and socialize, and it is more rewarding to sit down with their children after school or each night and help with their homework. That nighttime interaction can many times make the difference between an all "A" student and a poorly performing student.

If you have a demanding professional career, it is good to engage good quality tutors for your child. Mentors that will be there for them when you're not.

Many schools have on site YMCA programs where you child goes directly from school to a safe nurturing environment. This is affordable and well worth the investment in your child's future.

Prospective mothers must consider very carefully whether it is ok with you to get up as many as five times a night for your infant. This could go on as long as two years. Fatigue is a real issue here, especially if the mom has a high-powered day job.

Finances are an issue as well. Even diapers or diaper services are expensive. Is it ok with you not to have a spare penny for years? Is it ok that every time you do get a few bucks ahead, there are unexpected doctor bills from the colds your child will bring home from school and give to the entire family? Is it ok with you not to have any new clothes of your own in order that your child can have decent school clothes, which he will constantly grow out of or damage, rather than wear out!

Another important issue is the fact that children raised by working parents can only reach their full potential by the parent carefully replacing what the child is missing at home by paying for quality outside caregivers and tutors.

The caliber of nursery school care needed is a significant cost. A high-powered private school with after school care also generally requires a reservation AND DEPOSIT before the child is born. Can you afford this kind of expense, or are you going to have to rely on cheaper and less attentive care where your child will be more likely to be raised by other children. If this is the case it may be best to forgo having a family at this time. Wait till you have either more time or the money to provide properly for your children.

In many cases fate determines when you start your family. The fact that you are reading this book indicates you will do the best job you can raising your child or children.

Another consideration is how do you relate to your pets. This may seem off the track, but it is not. Do you get angry and resentful of the care they require? Do you take your daily frustration out on them? Do you kick your dog when you're mad? Keep your pet outside on a chain?

Do you forget to buy pet food?

5 IN THE WOMB

There's a more than 50% chance your pregnancy is unplanned. After all, not all of us are rocket scientists. Many beautiful families are created by accident. The fact that you are reading this book indicates that you have decided to become a parent and are concerned enough about your new child to educate yourself about parenting. You are embarking on an adventure that will last the rest of your life. Let's do it right!

PROTEIN

The Cedar Sinai Medical Clinic in Los Angeles suggests that a pregnant woman ingest (eat) 80 grams of protein per day along with the calcium, vegetables and fruit that are so important for your baby's proper development. If the parent can't afford to buy this much meat, soy protein powder is a good replacement as well as legumes (beans) and cottage cheese. The protein powder is good because the expectant mother can mix up a shake in the morning with all of her daily protein requirement.

According to the Cedar Sinai Prenatal Clinic, protein is crucial for brain development, especially in the last three months of pregnancy.

FRUIT

When your Gynecologist asks you if you are eating enough fruit, read between the lines. He's really saying that without the correct amount of fruit you will not move your bowels properly, and the poisons will stack up in your lower intestines and affect the health of the child you are carrying. This is a contributing factor in children that are prone to skin problems and rashes all the way through high school and into adulthood.

CALCIUM

If you hate milk, drink Calcium fortified orange juice. If you do not provide enough calcium, the baby will "borrow" it from you. Like the things most kids borrow from their parents, you will not get it back, and you will find your teeth cracking and falling out, not to mention bone deterioration (Arthritis and Osteoporosis).

A child deprived of calcium will also be prone to bone problems, and the agony and expense you will go through with the orthopedic department of your local Children's Hospital is a thousand times worse than making sure you get adequate calcium during pregnancy.

CIGARETTES AND ALCOHOL

Smoking restricts oxygen to the blood stream. If you smoke cigarettes when you are pregnant you can expect an underweight child with very possible brain damage, not to mention numerous other health problems such as asthma. Deprivation of oxygen affects all aspects of producing a healthy child.

Alcohol consumption can cause a malformation of the spine called Spina Bifida as well as many other physical and psychological syndromes. Spina Bifida is when the child is born with a portion of the spine exposed or damaged, generally causing loss of use of the legs, or in less major cases, lack of feeling in the lower limbs resulting in lifelong uncontrollable bowel movements. It is sometimes accompanied by curvature of the spine.

COCAINE

Mothers who use Cocaine are possibly condemning their children to brain damage, nerve damage and excessive health problems. There is a school of thought that cocaine usage in parents alters the brain and body chemistry causing ADD, Autism and Asperger's Spectrum in the off-spring.

Many of these "cocaine" babies become wards of the state, as the mothers have no desire, or are incapable of giving the babies the intense amount of care and attention they require.

At birth these infants must be detoxed, a heartbreaking procedure. Hard on the child and the parents. Autism is also a common result of a drug-abusing mother. Much more common than immunizations, which are in many cases blamed for autism but may, in fact, be blameless.

If you are an upwardly mobile yuppie who uses Cocaine socially, you should go to the local Children's Hospital and view the different birth defects that occur in the cocaine babies. With Cocaine it does not matter if you quit while you are pregnant. According to studies, the chromosomal damage is done in the parents during their cocaine use and lasts for life.

In any case, you should clean out your system before starting a family if you don't want to take a chance of having a child with numerous health problems that will be a psychological, physical and financial drain on you for life.

6 LISTEN TO YOUR FETUS

Even before birth, your child will express themselves. You will be able to communicate when your baby is big enough to make you feel their movement. At this point if you are in a position that is uncomfortable for your baby, your baby will kick.

Don't forget your baby will also kick for exercise, and so you must be perceptive. If you are lying on your back in bed, and not in an awkward position, your baby's kicks are most likely exercise. If you're bending over re arranging the closet under the sink, your child may be telling you they're squashed!

Sound can also affect a fetus. You may find excessive movement if you put a loud noise such as a kitchen blender too near your stomach. Try shutting it off to see if your baby calms down.

Music, however, is very important, especially the mother singing a song. Your baby will not care if you're on key or not, baby just knows it is mom. Baby will find it very soothing. You can give your child a head-start if you count numbers and repeat the alphabet when you're pregnant. Your child will always take comfort from the songs you sing to him in the womb. It's very calming.

Talk to your child, even before birth. The more you converse with your child, the more likely they will understand you after they are born. If you are lucky enough to be bi-lingual, speak in both or all languages you know. This will give your child a head-start later.

7 REST AND CRAVINGS

REST:

Get plenty of rest while you are pregnant and once your child is born. Take naps with your child, you both will need them. Don't be tempted to work while your child sleeps.

CRAVINGS:

In the last three months stay away from salt, it can kill you. If you have a craving for a certain kind of fruit, or any good food, eat as much as you crave. It's your body taking extra needed components. Each metabolism is different, and each pregnancy is different. This is why different moms crave different things. Be sure that your craving is a healthy one. A craving for sugar and sweets could indicate or even create a problem with diabetes in both you and your child.

Pay close attention to whether you are having a craving or are bored. A craving is your body telling you it needs some component of the food. If you are just bored, you will fight to get that weight off later.

With my first pregnancy I craved tart green apples. With my second I craved beef liver. I couldn't get enough of either. I have no idea what I was lacking that made me crave these foods. They are both foods I rarely if ever eat.

8 WHAT BABY WEIGHT

It is normal during pregnancy to gain around 35 pounds. This number depends on your stature in a non-pregnant condition.

In the old days, say all the way back to Neanderthal, it was necessary for the mother to also gain extra fat to convert into milk for the nursing infant.

Nowadays it is no longer a necessity to nurse the young, it is a choice. The new mother should decide whether they plan to nurse their young before birth and take steps to alter their diet and exercise if they don't plan to nurse. If the mother doesn't nurse, it is very difficult to lose the "baby weight".

As any mother will tell you, baby weight is hard to get off the body if not nursing.

The genetic stockpile for a pregnant mother is most often in the area of the thighs, buttocks. It also involves the front torso. It also depends on genealogy. Like mother, or grandmothers, like daughter.

Some mothers seem to snap back after birth to their pre-birth figures without effort, others seem to never fully shed the baby weight. This is usually genetic. Look at your siblings and female relatives to get an idea of what you are up against. Plan accordingly.

Just like skin color, weight accumulation has evolved to keep the infant alive. In areas of abundant food, the mother did not have to stockpile. In Areas where food is scarcer at times, the body evolved to stockpile more calories in preparation for feeding the newborn.

Genealogy is important. It is great that it is so readily available in this era of easy access to DNA and ancestry sites.

I am Irish; my ancestors survived the potato famine. Both times I was pregnant I blew up to resemble a potato and my metabolism is extremely slow. I attribute my family's survival of the famine to my genetically slow (efficient) metabolism.

9 DECORATING BABY'S ROOM

Commonly nurseries are decorated before the birth of the child. The initial design should last until the child is a toddler. Requiring convertible furnishings.

When the child is an infant, and therefore fairly immobile, a child depends on visual stimulation around the crib or playpen. In consideration of this, a parent might place a TV set in the nursery. Run Sesame Street on it. Even before the child can understand the words the moving pictures will stimulate brain growth and synapse connections. This gives a child a real head start on reading and numbers.

Be very careful not to play adult, or damaging themes on the nursery TV set. Your baby's brain is on its highest learning curve from 0 to 5 years old. Be aware even the nature shows have violent content. Be very careful even about the cartoons that your child sees.

THE SUBLIMINAL PARENT

Take your child out and about as much as possible.

Make sure you take your child to different places. Not just in a stroller around the block. All the visual and auditory input will help generate new synapse connections in your child's brain. This will accelerate their mental capabilities.

Cover the walls of the nursery with numbers, letters and real animals, planes, cars, anything you can think of. Don't put up a couple of bunnies and call it done.

In every position the infant should be able to look at and absorb something other than what the wallpaper companies think is appropriate. Why repeat a bunny ten thousand times when you can have many different images to look at.

Just make sure no image is frightening. All imagery should be subliminally positive. Help build character. Change out the imagery often. This will expand your child's synapses.

The number one most important element in your child's room is you and your spouse (or significant other). A warm smiling picture of both "parents" and other important "tribe" members should always hang near the child's bed for bonding and reassurance.

Color is a big consideration. For a calm environment do not decorate with red or any derivative of red, i.e.: Pink Purple etc. Regardless of what is fashionable. Though pink and blue are considered baby colors, the most nurturing color scheme is the one closest to mother's skin, beige. Green and blue are very calming, but cold. Beige is calm and yet warm at the same time. Throw in some light earth tones, if necessary. Let the wall and ceiling poster art be the color.

10 NURSING AND BABY BOTTLES

First, about milk.

Milk builds your child's bones. The amount of milk your child is given when an infant directly relates to your child's bone strength when older.

We all remember from our school days what children were prone to broken bones. A common reason for broken bones is lack of calcium when an infant. Very young infants should primarily drink milk. This gives them calcium and water and very important immunities if breast fed.

If the mother can't breast feed, give the closest thing to breast milk, goat's milk. Use formula as a last resort as it is laden with sugar and carbohydrates. Formula is reputed to be a significant contributing factor in juvenile diabetes.

A word about different baby bottles available. The plastic ones are the safest, except for one thing. They melt. DO

NOT leave them unattended on the stove in the sterilizer. If they melt they release very sickening, toxic fumes.

Glass bottles are easier to sterilize.

A new mom is always tired, be very careful not to blow up anything on the stove when you're catching an unexpected nap. Never lay down with the stove on!

Those cute bottles with the hole in the center are very labor intensive. They're hard to clean. If you use them you will need to increase your bottle clean up time by fifty percent.

The disposable bottle liners have the advantage of being sterile, and much easier to clean up. They also cause less ingestion of air, cutting down the burping and walking time.

Never leave your baby unattended with a bottle propped in their mouth. Your child can choke. Make sure your child's in a position where if they stop drinking the bottle will fall away from them.

Be aware that "Sippie" type cups have been found with disgusting mold inside the top apparatus. If you are going to use them, take them apart fully to clean.

Also be aware your child needs milk (formula) and water primarily. Juice is ok once in a while, but too much will rot teeth and contribute to obesity and diabetes. A young child never, ever, ever needs soda pop. The carbonation alone leeches calcium out of their bones. The average soda pop has 12 teaspoons of sugar per bottle.

11 TEETHING

Teething is your child's right of passage. For the same reason all puppies teethe

During teething your child's teeth are trying to break through their jaw and gums. The more you give them to chew on the better off they will be. The faster they will get through the process.

The teething process is on and off as the various teeth mature and need to break through.

Be aware they will be cranky. You would be too if you were going through that pain. They will also drool and in some cases run a fever.

The good news is that every baby will chew on whatever you put in its hand. It is your call whether that is a sugar filled "teething cracker" full of tartar, or a healthier rubber "Teething Ring".

A raw carrot is an option as long as you are careful that it is not a size your child can choke on.

In the old days, mothers would rub honey with brandy on the child's teeth to numb the pain. Not really a healthful option. In antique stores you sometimes find teething devices carved out of bone. Wood is not good because it can splinter.

When teething, an infant will drool, that is a good indicator that they are having some tooth pain. The more they can chew the faster the teething process will be.

A pacifier is not really hard enough to make much of a difference in breaking the new teeth through. A good firm rubber ring your infant can grasp is a nice choice.

Important! If your child is teething and seems to be in extreme pain, have your pediatrician check to make sure the tooth is coming in properly and not impacted or obstructed in any way. This may also show as an elevated temperature.

12 IS MY CHILD SICK

New parents don't have the experience to assess whether their child is sick. What you should look for:

1. Extreme Fussy-ness. If a child is coming down with something, the first evidence is sometimes extreme fussyness. If your child seems overly cranky, take their temperature. If the temperature is high call your pediatrician immediately.

2. Rosy Cheeks. A fever sometimes is first seen as rosy cheeks. Some children have naturally rosy cheeks all the time. If not, when you see rosy cheeks, take their temperature.

3. Diarrhea. This is very critical in young children. They can become de hydrated easily. The reason for the loose stool needs to be assessed. It could be the flu or something more serious. Call the pediatrician immediately.

4. Fever. In a young child a fever can deteriorate into something more serious very quickly. If the fever is really high put them in a cool bath while contacting your pediatrician.

5. Limp - unresponsive. There are several reasons for this. The most common is the child is too hot. The child may be overdressed for the weather. The child could be suffering from heat due to an overly covered stroller. It is tempting to dress a child very warmly to keep them more sedate. The parent must realize that when a child is too hot for long periods of time it can deteriorate mental acuity. If the child is limp and the temperature is elevated, then assess if the child is dressed too warmly. If not the cause, contact the pediatrician.

13 YOUR CHILD'S FIRST SHOT

It is good to train your child about shots and vaccinations before your child gets the first one.

Before going to the doctor show your child how it will feel. If you don't do this, it can be very traumatic, affecting your child for life.

Tell your child that he is going to get good stuff from the doctor that is going to protect him. Tell your child he will feel a tiny "dink".

Take your child's arm gently and tell your child, "I am going to show you what a dink is". Gently pinch your child's arm. Do it firmly enough that your child can feel it, but not hard enough to hurt them.

Say, "There, did you feel that? That is a dink!"

THE SUBLIMINAL PARENT

On the way to the doctor tell your child, "By the way, after your dinks, we are going to go for...." Here fill in the blank with your child's favorite thing. It could be ice cream, or the toy store, or if older, perhaps a movie.

According to Pediatric Craniofacial Surgeon, Dr, Larry Nichter, "children who are not aware of what a shot is have a tendency to be more and more traumatized each time they get a shot."

If the child knows he is going to get a "dink" or "tink" or whatever the parent chooses to call it, then the child will not be caught off guard and traumatized. Most likely the child will sit quietly and allow the dink in anticipation of the good stuff to follow.

Most Doctors do not see children very often that have been properly trained to expect the dink, so don't be surprised if you as the parent get some high praise.

14 WHAT'S THE BIG DEAL ABOUT WATER

You must remember at all times:

YOU are driving your child's car for the first years of their life. Because of that, it is important to know about WATER!

Water is the equivalent of oil in your child's car. It is the lubricant that carries the nutrients to all parts of your child's body.

Your child's brain is made up of synapses and very tiny capillaries. Without the proper amount of water, the blood is too thick, and the nutrients can't get out to all the capillaries in the brain and other parts of the body.

In order for the nutrients to travel all the way out to the end of those tiny capillaries, there needs to be water.

If your child is not drinking enough water, their blood becomes thick and the nutrients cannot get all the way out to where they need to be. You are restricting your child's brain development if you don't give them enough pure water.

There is a school of thought that lack of water, dehydration, may be a significant contributor to the advent of dementia in older adults.

This is an interesting theory.

What about fruit juices and soda? Isn't that water too?

No, with fruit juice there is water, but you are also putting a lot of sugar in your child's system. With soda there is water, but you are also serving your child carbonation, which leeches calcium for your child's bones, and sugar, which rots your child's baby teeth and prevents your child's adult teeth from coming in properly.

The sugar in fruit juice also contributes to juvenile diabetes.

An infant should occasionally have fruit juice for the vitamin C it provides. Do not make it your child's default drink.

Your infant should regularly drink milk and water. That is the best investment you can make in your child. If you feed formula, check the ingredients to make sure the formula you are feeding is not just made up of sugar of fructose. Don't put your child on the diabetes train.

A great alternative for mother's milk is goat's milk. You can get it from any good market, and it is very close in cellular structure to human breast milk. Be sure to shake it, some of the good stuff settles.

Initially you may have to request it from your grocer.

In the first few weeks of your child's life you should breast feed so that your child inherits your own immunities through the colostrum you will produce at that time. All your natural immunities will be in there.

Don't be bullied by other parents to let your child have soda or sugar laden treats too early. You will pay for this in dental bills and broken bones later, not to mention the effect on your child's brain development and physical energy.

Rarely do doctors talk to parents about hydration. Proper hydration is the major building block of your child's brain and musculature.

It is remarkable that most human beings do not drink enough water for their body to function properly. The average adult body is 50-65% water, averaging around 57-60%. The percentage of water in infants is much higher, typically around 75-78% water, dropping to 65% by one year of age. Fatty tissue contains less water than lean tissue. Fatty tissue is inert, does not contribute to the function of a healthy body.

Obesity can be caused by lack of hydration. As long as the body is dehydrated, it will feel hungry, crave intake. Sadly, the body does not define its cravings between water and food. What seems like hunger for food may be the body asking for a drink of water. Drinking the proper amount of water can stop hunger cravings. when you feel like a snack think about whether you have given your body enough water.

Unfortunately, most humans habitually eat a majority of

non-fluid based foods, causing the body to run in a constant dehydrated condition. This can mask as food craving resulting in overeating.

Also, very important, you or your child will become constipated without proper hydration. If there is not enough fluid in the body, the bowels cannot work properly. Fecal matter will build up in the lower intestine and literally poison the blood stream with old matter that should be expelled.

Not only will lack of hydration affect the blood, it affects the skin as well. If the skin does not have enough water hydration, it can result in lack of circulation causing bacteria to build up. This can result in severe acne and other skin aberrations and defects that are very traumatizing during puberty. It can cause premature aging of the skin.

Another symptom of dehydration are muscle cramps. If there is not enough hydration in the muscle tissue, it cannot operate properly.

If your child plays sports while dehydrated, they can experience crippling painful muscle cramps from lack of fluid in the muscle tissue. On a hot day they can be severely affected. They need to constantly replace what they are sweating out.

The good news here is that drinking pure water can quickly stop muscle cramps. It takes very little time for the body to distribute water intake.

The most important detriment of dehydration is in the classroom. Without the proper hydration, your child's brain development can be slowed or stunted. This will affect them for the rest of their lives. If your child is experiencing lack of focus, determine whether they are actually dehydrated before administering behavior masking drugs.

Pure water is the best hydration for a young child. Fruit juice contains sugar which affects the brain as well as the pancreas, it also can rot the teeth. Vitamin C is important, but fruit juice should not be the default drink for young children.

Children grow fast, they need calcium and water to feed the new cells they are creating every single day. Brain, bone and muscle.

Remember, sugar is addicting. If your give your child fruit juice or soda drinks, they will develop a craving for them. If you provide plenty of water, they will drink when they are actually thirsty.

Hunger is a symptom of both the need for food and for water. In many cases a child that over eats may actually needs water. It is the parent who trains the child to overeat. You drive the car, and you control what goes in it.

I know I am really stressing proper hydration in this chapter. It is very important!

If you start your child out with good hydration habits, they will develop all the brain cells, bone and muscle they require to be a well-oiled machine!

THE SUBLIMINAL PARENT

15 IS THIS REALLY COLIC?

There comes a time in an infant's life, it could be six weeks or later, that for some reason the child has a really hard time falling asleep. For the mothers that carry their babies in "Snugglies", it may not be noticeable in the daytime. A baby in a Snugglie is a happy relaxed camper. At night, however, when the baby is put down in the crib it may cry for hours until baby adjusts to how to go to sleep.

There is no easy way to get through this period. Likewise, a lot of colic at this age is misdiagnosed. Colic is a definite biological infant discomfort. The solution is generally thought to be walking the child. Many a parent has taken years off their life walking a child all night and having to work the next day. I call it the "walking dead".

If you believe your child has a problem with colic, check with your pediatrician. If there is no discernible health problem, "You put the baby down and let him cry himself to sleep." states respected Encino, California Pediatrician, Dr. Helen Lederer. She goes on to state, "It's ok to feel like you want to throw your child against the wall as long as you don't do it."

If you pick up your baby every time he cries, you are training your child to cry. Don't train your child to cry.

Remember, this is a developmental stage. The child is teaching itself how to fall asleep. Some have a harder transition than others. If you reward them for crying, they will never learn to go to sleep.

Sleep deprivation is a very serious disease of the parents of a newborn. What Dr. Lederer instructs her new parents gives them the space to express their exhaustion and frustration. She releases them from the guilt of letting their tiny newborn cry them-self to sleep. They are merely training themselves how to fall asleep.

Another wives trick that works very well is to turn on a vacuum in an adjacent room. The "white noise" it creates usually puts a baby to sleep quickly. There are also great white noise machines available. Just make sure it's at low volume so it does not affect your child's hearing. You won't need it long. The drive in the car also works, but you're just as likely to wake up the child when you get home; and have to start all over. The best solution is to just allow the child to train himself how to go to sleep.

The most important thing to remember is that this is just a developmental stage. It will end. Honest, it will.

16 ASSESSING YOUR CHILD'S CRIES

New mothers sometime have a hard time deciding when a cry is a need, or when a cry is just "fussy-ness". It's easy to rule out reasons your child is crying:

1. Diaper Change.

A quick inspection will tell mother if this is the reason

2. Hungry.

A child with a fast metabolism will require more food than one with a slow, efficient, metabolism. Mother will become familiar with her child's needs and be able to estimate when the next bottle will be needed.

3. Uncomfortable.

Check your child for any clothing that may be tangled, a pin, or if the child is too hot or too cold. Too hot exhibits as sweaty or flushed or limp. Cold exhibits as shivering or cold to the touch.

4. Sick.

Is the child flushed, and running a temperature? Are their cheeks red? Sometimes you will see red cheeks and hear a tired cry before you are aware your child is sick. If your child is really fussy, they may be coming down with something.

5. Attention.

Children are smart. It is easy for a mother to teach them to cry for attention. If the mother carries their infant in a Snugglie® type sling there is never need for the child to cry in order to be held. Children in Snugglie® type devices are much less likely to suck their thumbs or require a "pacifier".

17 CRIB DEATH

A very frightening thing to confront as a new parent is Crib Death (SIDS aka Sudden Infant Death Syndrome). In the past a big mystique had built up around the fact that a child could just, for no apparent reason, stop breathing.

Studies in the last few decades have shown that although SIDS still is a big mystery, a large amount of the parents who before had attributed their child's death to SIDS, have now come forward and admitted that the death was actually caused by a pillow in the crib, cute fluffy side padding, or a quilt which the infant was inadvertently smothered by. This is a devastating thing for a parent to have to confront.

It must be absolutely life changing to carry the burden of guilt for your own child's death all by yourself. Luckily there are support groups springing up for parents who have inadvertently, with absolutely no intention, smothered their own children.

In the blink of an eye an infant can turn himself face down into a pillow. You know, the one grandma insisted on putting into the crib. If you're out of the room for a few minutes you've lost your child.

The safest way to dress a sleeping child is in jammies warm enough to circumvent the need for a blanket, and NO pillow. Use thin padded sides for the crib, not fluffy soft ones that the child can inadvertently bury its face in.

Do not use ill-fitting sheets in the crib. Use a nice tight fitted crib sheet.

18 THE FAMILY BED

A WARNING

It has lately been discovered that sleeping with a baby in bed can be dangerous for the baby if there is not enough room for breathing space around the baby. There have been reported cases where a parent has rolled over and smothered the infant, or the infant sleeps with its face in the parent's side and does not get enough oxygen. This can cause brain damage or death.

In a natural setting with no human assistance, after a baby is born it will climb up the mother and nurse naturally.

If God had not intended the infant to sleep with the mother, he would have made other feeding provisions. The ultimate in efficiency is to breast feed and allow the infant to share the parent's bed. It is definitely easier to just roll over in your sleep and allow the baby to nurse, than it is to go to a different room, and on the way perhaps have to prepare a bottle.

Put yourselves in your baby's shoes. Where would you rather wake up, in a cold empty, huge room, All BY YOURSELF, or snuggled up with your mom and dad. If mom and dad feel like getting rowdy, they can go to the den or the guest room. Isn't that a small price to pay for the indelible family bonding?

If you do eave your baby on a bed, be sure they cannot fall off inadvertently.

Studies have shown that in the countries where it is the custom to share the family bed with those children that wish to, the families are much more bonded to each other. When the children feel secure enough, they will leave on their own accord, opting for their own space.

After the child has left the family bed for a more independent situation, don't be surprised if he needs to return occasionally. There could be insecurities bothering him that aren't apparent.

If your child is showing a need to be close, try to get him to open up about what is bothering him. Sometimes all it takes is a sympathetic ear to relieve the pressure, or at least make it more bearable. At all times assure your child that you love him, and you do enjoy being close to him.

Children who are allowed to sleep with the parent also are less likely to be thumb suckers, as they are allowed to hold onto their parent as long as necessary to reinforce their feelings of security. Thumb sucking, as discussed later, is a symptom of lack of parental physical closeness.

Before a child can talk, body language is necessary to reassure him. If he spends his life in strollers and cribs, he will need to find a replacement for mother's warmth, usually the thumb or pacifier.

The "Snugglie" and the family bed are the most powerful ways to raise a secure child who does not need to suck his thumb.

THE SUBLIMINAL PARENT

19 THE TERRIBLE TWOS

The "Terrible 2s" is a very significant learning spurt for your child. It is a huge leap in brain development

Overnight your child discovers the concept and power of the word "no". No is a word that you have been using to prevent certain behavior in your child. All of a sudden, the child will say it to the parent when the parent gives a command.

In order to avoid the response of "No" at this time the parent can rephrase the command. Instead of saying, "Come to the table" for example, say I am going to the table and immediately turn and walk to the table. Children generally will follow. "Now I am going to sit in my chair." Help your child get into his chair.

During this transitional period avoid asking your child if he wants to do something. Many times, during this period, even if he does want to do it, he will say "No!"

When frustrated, the parent needs to remind themselves that their child's brain is developing. The child's answers may be confused; the child may answer in a way they do not intend.

20 CHOOSING CHILD CARE

In this era of the obligatory dual working household, as well as the many single parent families, childcare is generally a must. Before a parent decides to put his child into a childcare situation there are some important things that have to be considered.

The main consideration is; do you want another individual to raise your child? One must realize that no matter how much "quality time you give your child in the morning and at night, the individual who cares for you child during the day will have an indelible impact on that child's habits and morals.

Be aware the childcare individual will be taking the majority of responsibility for your child's mental development as well as toilet training etc. A parent can set all the policy, but it is the caregiver who must follow through. You will not be there to make sure your wishes are being followed.

Is the caregiver concerned about health and fitness? What type of food will they offer your child? Will they give your child sweets during the day, even if you have instructed them not to? Will they smoke around your child? Will your child be breathing secondary smoke all day long?

The thing a parent MUST accept about secondary care givers is that no matter what you ask them to do regarding the care of you child, they are most likely, the minute you drive away down the street, to care for your child the way they think best.

The other thing to carefully consider, especially parents from upper middle class and above economic situations, is who is your child bonding with?

A lot of professional parents, households of two high powered working parents, are proud of the fact that they can afford live in help. It allows them to work in the day and go to all the requisite social functions at night. They must accept the fact that although they are the biological parents, it is more likely that the child will bond with the live in. That person will be the one who is around to kiss the boo boos, give the rockies and tell the bedtime stories.

Don't be surprised or angry when your child goes to this person instead of you for comfort if he has a choice. Also be very careful that the person you choose to provide twenty-four-hour care for your child is someone you respect, and someone you would not mind your child growing up like, because YOUR CHILD WILL.

Amazingly, it is the less affluent families which often end up with the highest quality care many times. The affluent parent, many times will secure someone to live in to live in and provide childcare based on cost. On the positive side, in many cases, the child will grow up to be bi-lingual, with a respect for different cultures. On the downside, the child might be raised watching soap operas and cigarette smoke, whether in English or some other language. In this respect the less moneyed parent that puts his child in a good communal childcare environment may be more likely to get the kind of care, nurturing and education the child needs

In the old days the mother or grandmother spent time each day working with the children, helping them learn numbers and letters and reading them stories. Now the good childcare centers fill these needs without usurping the affection away from the parents. Because it is their sole occupation, the childcare centers can focus on the child's development much better than a mother who also has to run a household and work for a living.

How many of us come home from a full day's work with the energy to not only fix dinner, but also teach the children well? We're lucky to have the energy to cook a meal, do laundry and clean up the kitchen before falling into bed.

Nowadays a parent has a choice of Montessori, Kindercare and many other types of childcare care centers. If the income is low, the county will assist in childcare expense. One of the best after school programs for school age children is the YMCA. They pick the children up directly from school and take them to a safe nurturing environment. The YMCA not only offers the kids a varied activity schedule, but homework assistance as well. The YMCA also has a good pre-school childcare program. The Boys and

Girls Clubs are also good options for after school care.

Be aware there are several childcare companies who pride themselves that they allow the children to choose what activities they want to do. In theory this sounds great, but it is a nightmare when the child is integrated into a traditional school environment. The child is used to doing whatever activity they want at times they choose. This is not an option in regular kindergarten and can be very disruptive.

The important thing in choosing a childcare center is not only cleanliness, but do the children look happy and well nourished? Can you walk in unannounced at any time? Are all the areas clearly accessible? What types of food do they encourage the parents to send to school? What does it smell like?

A nursery school that allows junk food and sugary treats in the child's lunch box should be avoided. This type of care center will show up on the children's faces. They will have bad skin color, a tendency to overweight, bad teeth and dark circles under their eyes. Due to bad diet, the children will also have a tendency to misbehave at the center, increasing the chance that the caregivers will be cranky with them.

Make sure the children at the childcare center are happy, bright and alert, gregarious and in good physical condition. Any fear denotes less than optimum care.

Another consideration is the ratio of caregivers to children, are kids raising kids? If there are more than seven children per caregiver, there is a possibility that your child will not be consistently guided and nurtured, and he may tend to just absorb the habits of the other children he spends his day with. If this is the case, the parent better make sure the children his child is spending the day with behave appropriately.

Another important consideration is whether the caregivers communicate with the children easily. Will your child be treated firmly but with respect? Some "childcare" situations are merely individuals who want to justify staying home, or simply need the money and have no interest in actually enhancing the development of their clients. They may merely in it "for the money".

When choosing a childcare situation, you must also decide whether you wish to have your child in a progressive learning situation, or a more play-oriented environment.

You have the car, the driver's license, and the checkbook. The kind of personal care you child will have is entirely in your hands.

※ THE SUBLIMINAL PARENT

21 WHAT'S THE DEAL ABOUT DIAPERS

Disposable diapers are extremely convenient. You take it off, fold it like a little present and throw it away. It keeps baby drier and your child is less likely to have diaper rash.

If you prefer not to contribute to the landfills you can use cloth diapers. You will either wash them yourself if you are a stay at home mom or have a nanny that is on board, or you will have a diaper service.

The advantage with cloth diapers is that your child will toilet train earlier. That saves a LOT of money!

You must realize that children change behavior when THEY want to, usually because they are uncomfortable.

Disposable diapers and "Pull Ups" are NOT uncomfortable. They do not get cold and clammy. There is no motivation for a child to toilet train. A cloth diaper, on the other hand, gets cold and clammy when there is urine present. They get heavy and droop.

When disposable "Pull Ups" hit the market the day care providers HATED it. Instead of children toilet training at 1 to 2 years old, all of a sudden, toddlers were not toilet training until 5 years old! It was a boon for the disposable manufacturers. A true sucking black hole for the pocketbooks of the parents, and horribly labor intensive for the preschool day care centers!

My mother used to brag about how early I toilet trained. My older sister claims it was because my mother never changed my diapers. My sister was expected to do it at only two years older than I. I have recollections of wearing cold soggy diapers hanging down to my knees to this day. Of course I toilet trained early!

22 EFFORTLESS TOILET TRAINING

The easiest way to toilet train is Subliminally.

Let's analyze what makes a child want to toilet train himself. You notice I say train himself? That's because your child is the ONLY one in the room who can choose NOT to poop or pee in his pants.

The motivating reason for a child to cease the need for a diaper is very simple. Discomfort. No stay-dri training pant can motivate a child. They are not uncomfortable.

What motivates a child not to soil his pants is the knowledge that if he does, he gets to sit around in not only a soggy or poopy CLOTH training pant, but his clothes will be soggy as well. Children are smart, much smarter that most of us give them credit for. If they know that taking a pee or a poop in their pants is going to make them soggy and gross, hey, they will make a concerted effort not to do it. WHEN THEY ARE READY.

Since the advent of the "stay-dri disposable training pant" the nursery schools are finding themselves having to diaper kids till they are four and five years old. Ridiculous, and incredibly expensive for the parent.

The industry has all but made cloth training pants obsolete. They can be found online but are expensive. As much as 18us dollars a pair!!! If you are creative, you can modify a cloth diaper easily into a training pant with an elastic waist. Much cheaper to buy a pack of diapers and modify them than paying a fortune for one single training pant. The good news is they don't wear out. you can pass them on when you no longer need them.

Nursery schools surveyed said that the change in the age of toilet training is directly attributable to the advent of "stay dri" training pants that do not discomfort the child. What possible motivation is there? It's much easier to just wet your pants than it is to have to go to the bathroom.

At toddler age few children can easily manipulate their own clothing. It's a big hassle to go to the bathroom. However, when the alternative is to have to stand around in wet soggy clothing, guess what? The motivation is there!

Before starting out on toilet training however, the parent must consider this:

There is a very specific time when each child is physically and psychologically ready to toilet train himself, he will not train successfully if forced to do so too early. Early punishment associated with premature toilet training can cause a child to stutter.

Each child is different. Some toilet train early, some late. There is no rule, and no right or wrong age. Once the parent feels ready to toilet train, the parent must determine if the child is ready.

Once you feel your child may be ready to toilet train, do the following:

Each morning hold up a diaper in one hand, and a CLOTH training pant in the other hand. Say to your child, "do you want a diaper or big (girl/boy) pants today? The child will initially choose the cloth training pants wanting to be a big (girl/boy). Put them on saying, "When you wear big Girl/Boy pants you have to use the potty, so tell me when you have to go to potty and I will help you."

Be prepared the first few times with a change of clothing and a diaper, plus some clean up materials. Soon your child will have to go to the bathroom. An accident WILL occur. Don't be too speedy noticing the child has wet himself. Give him a chance to truly "experience" the discomfort.

When your child makes you aware that they are soiled (and probably crying about it) be sympathetic. Say, "Oh, you forgot to tell me to take you to the potty!" CHEERFULLY clean your child up, and then put him in diapers again for the rest of the day.

The next day give your child the choice again. Your child is smart, remember, you child knows that if he is wearing the big boy/girl pants, and wets, it will be gross. Each time your child chooses the CLOTH training pants, be prepared for an accident. You will find, however, that the child will go back to the diaper for a while, and then he will start choosing the "big boy pants" and cease having accidents. Children want to be big girls and boys.

THIS IS VERY IMPORTANT.

DO NOT TO EGO OUT ON HOW YOUNG YOUR CHILD TOILET TRAINS.

It is not uncommon for children forced to train too early to have problems with fear of lack of control. Many times, this fear leads to stuttering if trained before they are physically or psychologically ready. Never, ever, spank your child for soiling themselves. This can cause irreparable psychological damage.

Also think about this. It is easier to wait till the child is ready, and continue to diaper him, than to force him into a behavior that makes twenty times the work for you. A forced behavior that can keep you in a state of misdirected anger at you child. It's easier to change a diaper than to have to completely wash and redress your child.

When your child is ready to train, accomplish it quickly by allowing him to wear training gear that allows him to feel soggy. If you do this it will be over quickly, and on to the next!

The invention of the stay-dry pull-ups has been a gold mine for the diaper manufacturers. The parents and caregivers get the shaft.

23 ENFORCING NO

As early as possible, a child must understand the word "NO" for their own safety.

When they are is tiny infant, if you do not wish your child to do something, gently stop them and say 'no'. Be consistent with your training. Other mothers will look on in wonder when your child accepts your first no in the checkout line where the smart store always chooses to put the candy. How many times have you seen a mother give in to a screaming child after two or three Nos?

The mother of the screaming child has set herself up for failure. She has created her own ongoing nightmare. The nightmare began because at some point she found it was easier, less embarrassing, to give in to her child than to stick to her NO.

It's not easy to stand firm in the face of an embarrassingly screaming tearful child reaching out pitifully for a candy bar or toy. There's always some Grannie in line murmuring, "Oh, just let the poor thing have the treat Dearie!"

At some point the loving parent will have to be prepared to look like a jerk and drag a crying child out of a store without the candy or toy. Isn't one or two of those incidents worth having a child who will accept no the first time, and happily go on to his next thoughts, over a child that creates a scene every time he wants something, and won't take no for an answer?

Remember, YOU are the one who creates/controls the behavior of your child.

Here's the drill: even before your child can talk, he is able to reach out and cry for something. At this point you must gently pull his hand back and say "no". Then you MUST ignore any further crying or reaching.

THIS IS VERY IMPORTANT!

You are training your child that you mean what you say. You are training your child to respect the rules. The parent that says three "Nos" and then lets the child have the item in question just to shut him up, is training the child that if he cries long enough, he will win. They are teaching their child to misbehave. That parent is creating their own nightmare. That's not going to make your parental day! It is also not going to help the child be a success later in life.

When pulling the child's hand away, it is NOT necessary to slap the little hand. Repeated GENTLE hand restraint until the child quits the action, or you are loading him in the car, is what is required.

Have a stiff upper lip. Every parent has to suffer one or two embarrassing screaming incidents in order to train the well-behaved child. Just close your ears to the 100 decibels. Picture a child who minds on the first no, that's what you're building!

YOU MUST WIN, DO NOT GIVE IN!

If you are consistent, your child, who is quite bright, will quickly learn that what you say is what is. It will be a waste of energy for him to cry, and he won't. By the same token, if you tell your child he can do something, no matter how inconvenient it is, you MUST follow through.

Your child is learning how to behave from you. If you don't keep your word, why should he? Remember children learn subliminally by watching your actions.

Your child will know that if you say he can do something, he can. He will also know that if you say no, it is no, PERIOD. You will never have to carry him screaming from a store once he knows the rules. That doesn't mean your child won't ask for things, they will. But they will accept what you say, and you will be proud of your child and yourself in the face of all the other children you will see misbehaving in the checkout line.

The Exception…

If you say <u>MAYBE</u> to your child, your child will know he can continue to persuade, but once you say no, the issue will be over. Because of this, your child will be a joy to be with.

Don't ever say no to your child if you haven't decided yet if you will let them have their wish. Say maybe. When you decide then say no or yes… and stick to it!

24 HOW TO MANAGE A TANTRUM

As your child's parent, it is your job to train your child that a tantrum does not work as a tool to get what they want. This will save you, the parent years of embarrassment.

The parent must understand that they will have an immediate "flight or fight" reaction to a screaming child. The parent's immediate reaction is to do whatever is necessary to stop the child from his angst.

This is how tantrum behavior is enabled.

This is the worst thing you can do. At the very first instance, you cannot cave and give your screaming, kicking child what your child wants to stop him. If you do this, you are SUBLIMINALLY TRAINING your child that a screaming, kicking tantrum is a working scenario for them to control you.

THE SUBLIMINAL PARENT

You are teaching them how to control you!

You must prepare yourself for embarrassment the first time it happens, to save your relationship with your child. Also, to save your child's relationship with the world around him.

When your child commences with screaming and/or rolling on the floor kicking their feet, you must just calmly walk away. If at home, immediately go into a different area and totally ignore your child's tantrum. Ignore him for as long as it takes him to collect himself.

You need to teach your child IMMEDIATELY that this behavior DOES NOT WORK. Remember, children learn the quickest between 0 and 5 years old. Once they learn that a screaming, kicking tantrum does not work they will stop the behavior.

A restaurant is a good example of this. If you immediately remove your child to the car for misbehaving in a restaurant, you are SUBLIMINALLY TRAINING your child that if he is ever bored and doesn't want to sit still, all he needs to do is throw a fit and you will take him outside and spend time with him,

Instead you need to gently, but forcefully keep him in his place until the fit stops. Your child will quickly learn there is no payoff here and the behavior will stop.

You must be willing to be embarrassed one or two times in public to avoid years of agony. Just ignore the looks of the bystanders who don't understand.

25 WHY YOUR CHILD WON'T EAT

Keep track of your child's body rhythm. When your child seems to be hungry all the time, ("What do you mean you're hungry, we just had dinner!"), the chances are he is getting ready for a large growth surge and his body is stockpiling.

At this time, it is imperative that your child have enough calcium, protein and other nutrients. So often we see children TRAINED out of a preference for milk by their parents, when their bones haven't finished growing.

It's so sad to watch a mother feeding an infant soda pop in a baby bottle, when the only thing that should be entering that child is milk or water and occasionally fruit juice (this can rot their teeth if given too often). It is a proven fact that carbonated water leaches calcium from the bones.

If your child doesn't seem to want to eat, don't force him. Put his leftover plate in the refrigerator so your child can go back for it when hungry again.

After the stage where a lot of food is ingested, the body will need lots of rest, and much less food. Your child's appetite will go away temporarily. If you're worried about your child not eating, take him to your pediatrician for a checkup. If the doctor says your child is in good health, just let your child control the quantity (not quality) of his intake.

Remember, a child will crave food until all his nutritional needs are met. If you feed your child a lot of the wrong fast, or junk foods, the child will crave more food than if you allow him to eat good healthy food.

Never force-feed your child. Your child knows what quantity they need to eat. If you force them to overeat you are creating a child with no stop button. They lose the ability to judge how much they need to eat.

The worst thing for your child's health is to make them "clean their plate". Put the plate back in the fridge and when they are hungry again, they will let you know. Give it back to them then.

It is also a good idea to keep a tray of healthy snacks in the fridge. Such as broccoli, carrots, chicken nuggets, etc. Good finger food that they can have any time they feel hungry.

Many times parents comment, "I'm a single working parent, I barely have the energy to take my child to McDonalds in the evening." It's ok to take your child to McDonalds. At McDonalds choose for your child the more powerful foods on the menu. ALWAYS milk, water or orange juice, NOT soda pop. Avoid the greasy French fries that are so unhealthy and addictive.

Your child can abuse his teeth, bones and kidneys with colas later. If you give your child too much juice, soda pop or other sugary drinks you will rot their baby teeth and their adult teeth will not come in properly. That sets your child up for heartache later or a really big orthodontist bill down the road.

If your child's taste in food has been properly instilled when young, he will prefer the chicken nuggets or chef's salad to the hamburger or French fries. Sliced apples are a great alternative to French-fries.

An excellent meal at McDonalds is the grilled chicken sandwich. It can be ordered with no sauce (contains sugar). A mom can even cut up the grilled chicken for a toddler. That with the bun, lettuce and tomato and a carton of milk make a very good meal. Just forgo the ketchup and mayonnaise. They are both almost 90% sugar.

Remember, you are in charge of what your child eats. You have the money and the power. The buck stops with you.

At all times remember, you are much bigger, and the child will do as you say unless you have trained your child to scream for what he wants. If your child has been assisted in developing a taste for greens, he will enjoy the chef's salad which is as good as something you can fix at home, containing chicken, cheese and the important veggies. These are an extremely well-balanced meal for a growing child.

When your child is very young, he will chew on whatever

you hand him. It's your choice to hand him a cookie full of sugar or a stalk of broccoli or some parsley. That early you are building your child's good habits subliminally.

If your child wants a kid's meal for the toy, which is most times the case, buy the toy ala carte. They will sell it alone. This allows the child to have what he wants, and the parent the ability to provide a good customized meal.

Do not make your child finish the meal to get the toy. If your child is full, save the rest of the meal for later. Never ever make your child eat more than they want at a sitting They know what they need. Better to let them come back for more later when they actually are hungry.

Children not only love finger foods, they can easily manipulate them. Remember, young children will put whatever you hand them into their mouth. This is subliminal parenting.

When children are young they put everything in their mouth. You are the one who determines what that is. Instead of a sugary cracker, give them a carrot, broccoli or a piece of fruit. Prepare it with no dressing and let the child pick what he wants.

NEVER MAKE YOUR CHILD CLEAN HIS PLATE IN ORDER TO GET DESSERT.

In fact, when young, avoid dessert for your child. They do not need the empty, addictive calories. if fed properly with good food, your child will eat as much as he requires. Save the sugary treats for Sunday, or Friday night at the movies or perhaps a once a week trip to Baskin Robbins. Or never if you really want a healthy fit child.

DO NOT leave sugary treats about the house. We unconsciously eat them regularly, having no clue the quantity of our intake. With the generally sedentary lifestyles we live in nowadays there is no use metabolically for sugar every day, we can't burn it off, it just stockpiles.

THE PAVLOV TRUCK

That's the most appropriate name for the neighborhood ice cream truck. Not so common now as in years past. Now it has been replaced by the corner 7/11.

Parents teach their children at an early age that when they hear the ice cream truck bell they are to come running into the house begging for money for a treat. If the parent says no, an unpleasant scene is sure to follow. One can avoid the whole syndrome by NEVER starting to buy your child items from the ice cream man. Just don't do it. They don't need the sugar in any case.

These days that translates to the 7/11.

If your child is not in the habit of buying items off the ice cream truck, there will be no trauma as it passes through the neighborhood. Make sugary treats an outing, not a conditioned response.

At all times remember ice cream induces a sugar high, and then a crash. If your child is a sugar sensitive, he needs to be given ice cream only in a situation where the subsequent hyperactivity and following temper tantrum and tears can do no harm. The parent must take responsibility.

THE SUBLIMINAL PARENT

Remember the parent is the purveyor of the drug. When the child misbehaves, the parents must remind themselves that it was their willingness to let the child have the treat that has created the misbehavior. The parent is the enabler of the misbehavior, the child's sugar drug dealer.

26 ABOUT BULLYS AND BULLYING

Long before your child goes to school you must educate them about bullies. This is the only way to protect them.

The parent must let their child know that they should feel sorry for bullies. Let the child know that kids who are bullies do it because they feel bad about themselves. Bullies feel that they are not worthwhile and are mean to other kids because they are very sad inside.

Let the child know that the bully is not being mean because they don't like your child. They are being mean because they feel insecure and lonely. Tell them also many times bullies pick on kids because the child has something, they wished they had. Sometimes they pick on kids because they are being picked on or abused at home.

If the parent has armed the child with the truth before they meet their first bully, then the child has a chance of surviving the bullying. Both physically and psychologically.

What to do if your child is being bullied.

There is no excuse for the school or caregiver to allow bullying. If a child is bullied to the point of wanting to or actually hurting themselves, the bully should be held responsible. They should be held just as responsible as if they had shot the child with a gun or hit them with a rock. The parent needs to seek out the highest authority and demand that the bully be removed if not arrested.

The law needs to change about school bullying. The bullies AND their parents need to be held accountable. Bullying is a crime.

27 A PARENT'S RESPONSIBILITY

A few decades ago, legislation was passed that prevented teachers from disciplining students in the classroom. Prior to that, if a boy acted badly, he went to see the coach and got paddled. If a girl acted up it was not unheard of for her to get her knuckles rapped sharply with a ruler.

This discipline by the teacher/coach kept the classrooms in order. Whether the parent had properly trained their child or not, the child learned quickly not to misbehave in the classroom. Children are smart. They learn quickly not to do things that do not benefit them. At that time, classrooms, by and large, were quiet. Learning could happen.

Nowadays the public-school teacher has absolutely no power to keep their classroom quiet and organized. Nowadays the inmates are running the asylum. Because of that, it is an imperative responsibility of the parent to properly train their children to respect authority and behave responsibly prior to entering school.

Teaching your child to respect authority is for their own benefit. If their classroom is too disrupted to conduct education your child is being cruelly cheated.

It is the parent's responsibility to make their best effort to send their child to a school ready to learn. It is also a parent's responsibility to send their child to the best school available. A school where focused learning actually is accomplished. Avoid schools where the inmates are running the asylum.

28 PACKING YOUR CHILD'S LUNCH

When packing your child's lunch remember, you are building a successful child. What goes into the lunch box is the gas your child will run on and what will build your child's car. You must build a child who will be there to take care of you when you are too frail to take care of yourself. Think long term, not just for today.

In light of that, look at your child's lunch as your child's gas tank. The quality of the gas you put into it will build your child, allow your child to grow and develop properly.

If your child has a slow (efficient) metabolism, your child will need much less food that a child with a fast (inefficient) metabolism. (Fewer calories, more veggies) A child with a slow metabolism retains food value much more efficiently than a child with a fast metabolism. A fast metabolism pushes the food rapidly through the system. It does not give the child's system enough time to stockpile all the nutrients.

THE SUBLIMINAL PARENT

The child with a fast metabolism will be slimmer, seem to always be naturally hungry. This child will need more calories to maintain a healthy weight.

"I don't know how Marie can eat so much and stay so slender!" Marie has a fast, inefficient metabolism.

We say naturally hungry here because often the parent will train their child to constantly eat out of boredom, not out of actual need. Remember, you are a Subliminal Parent. What you do your child will copy.

If you snack all day long out of addiction or boredom, there is a good chance your child will do that as well. You are setting them up for obesity either now or when their system slows down at around age 25.

Remember this when you pack your child's lunch for day care or school. Packing a cookie or a candy bar is not a way to show love to your child. It is a way to addict them to sugar and condemn then to a life of obesity and depression.

Pack the main lunch of "good gas", such as a sandwich and piece of fruit, in the lunchbox as well as additional nutritious finger foods you child can enjoy later if they feel hungry. You can pack more good foods than sugary foods.

Remember, crackers such as "Goldfish" turn directly to sugar while they are still in your child's mouth. Avoid hollow foods such as this type of bad gas.

Always give your child good building blocks, "good gas", whether at home or away.

29 WHAT IS SCHOOL FOR

Most children have no idea why they are going to school, other than "To Learn Stuff".

A best-kept secret is that many parents don't give any thought about why their children are in school. Most parents are so relieved to have the child finally in school that they forget to really think about:

WHY ARE THEY IN SCHOOL?

The short answer is:

"THE MORE YOU KNOW, THE LESS YOU TOW!

The more productive answer is: "the better you do in school, the more awesome stuff you can have!"

Or how about this answer (My favorite, but hard for a young child to get their head around): When I am old and can't take care of myself, you will be able afford to take good care of me!"

Your child is not in school just to get good grades you can brag about. Your child is in school to learn how the world works.

<u>Your child needs to understand that if they don't do their work, they don't get a paycheck.</u>

In school the paycheck is grades. In the real world the paycheck is money. It allows your child to pay rent, buy food and buy a car and go on vacation. It allows them to take their girl or boyfriend on a nice date. It allows them to support their own family.

Young children are not yet able to appreciate how important retirement funds are, that will hit them in middle age unless you let them participate in helping you build your retirement. That gives them a head start on reality.

Make your child aware of what you do to help your parents when they are retired and enter old age. They will view that as appropriate adult behavior. They will do it for you without question when you need it!

If you don't pay much attention to your retirement, then your child basically becomes your retirement. They will be taking care of you when you no longer can. Their capability to take care of you directly relates to how well they did in school. Does your child know how the world works?

You are creating the quality of your own future by how well you allow our child to learn how to make his world work.

30 HOMEWORK PRACTICES

Doing homework is a learned habit. Like all habits, when ingrained, it becomes automatic.

The ideal is if there is a stay at home parent that can sit their children at the kitchen or dining room table as soon as they are home from school and help them complete all their homework. Build an awesome habit.

When the child gets home from school and finds a nice, nutritious snack waiting for them on the "homework" table there is a positive association. The parent can ramp it up a notch and bring in some real-world training. They can pick a reward for each page of homework done 100% CORRECT by their child. (Not done by the parent!)

In our house it was a dollar a page for **<u>100% CORRECT</u>**. Followed by a trip to Toys-R-Us on the weekend with their "paycheck".

For young children the reward has to be immediate, tangible. A glass "pay" jar on the counter works well so the child can see the reward. A special child I tutored was an avid video gamer, so I bought a bag of tokens from his favorite arcade. That meant more to him than money.

Once your child has developed a habit of sitting down right after school with a nice snack and their homework, it will become a lifelong practice.

The parent might also change the word "homework" to just "work". That way it is apples and apples with the real world. "What work do you need to do today?"

The parent even can give promotions for really good work. Promotions such as a nice poster for their room of their favorite thing. For financially challenged parents you can grab the picture online and print it out. Or an extra trip to the park.

The earlier your child understands good work equals good pay, the more chance they have for success when they are an adult.

31 WHEN SHOULD YOUR CHILD HAVE A PET

A pet is a wonderful way to "Subliminally Parent". Many times, a parent allows a child to have a pet when the child assures the parent: "I will take care of him!"

Too often the parent doesn't allow the child to live up to this. Taking care of a pet requires daily responsibility and many times the parent takes over the care out of convenience.

The parent does not allow the child to live up to his promise. This does a disservice to the child. If you take over responsibility for the pet, you are cheating your child out of a really important learning opportunity.

Taking care of their pet teaches them how to be responsible. On the other hand, if the parent steps in and does the pet care out of convenience, the parent is telling the child they do not have to live up to their agreements. This behavior will be carried over to all the child's responsibilities.

What the parent does for their own convenience now will create a child who assumes everyone will allow them to shirk their responsibilities.

This teaches their child that they don't need to keep promises or commitments.

At first if the child is very small, help them do their pet chores, but do not just do them for your child.

Praise your child; "Wow you did that just like a big girl/boy!" Children love to be big girls and boys. It's quite a motivator.

32 PARENTING A SPECIAL CHILD

Parenting a Special Child, whether he is Downs, Autism Spectrum, ADD or in a wheelchair, can be a very wearing life on the parents.

The parent has to be on guard at all times when the child is young to defuse and protect the child from the ignorant, hurtful behavior and comments of others.

In public people usually do one of two things, they stare at the child, or pretend the child is invisible, he doesn't exist.

Put yourself in the child's place. Say you go into a room and no one will look at you or talk to you. Even worse you catch people looking at you, but the minute they see you looking at them they look away.

The alternative is the person who stares at you without acknowledging you as a human being. You could be a tree.

Only when you've been on the receiving end do you realize; special people are human beings! They like to talk to people. When they get on an elevator, they appreciate a smile from the person who moves to let them on. They really want human contact. They want someone to look into their eyes and acknowledge their humanity.

In consideration of this, a parent of a severely challenged child will at times be invisible to the rest of the world. As the autistic child stands there in a screaming tantrum in the supermarket others will walk by as if you aren't there. The exception is the inevitable person who thinks you are beating the child, gives you their unwanted two cents.

You cannot change the world. You can keep the balance by making sure the next time you get in an elevator with a special person that you look him in the eye and smile, and comment on what a nice or rainy day it is. Give yourself, it will help make up for all the times you and your special child will be invisible.

33 THE CHILD ACTOR

Before allowing your child to entertain a career as a child actor there are things you need to carefully consider:

The Coach

In order to succeed in entertainment, it is no different than sports. You need a REALLY good coach. Acting coaches for children are expensive. Some who say they are coaches are really only glorified babysitters. With these you are throwing money away.

The real coaches, the successful ones, are not cheap. For a top coach you can expect to pay as much as $250 to $500 per month. You can pay as much as $120 per hour. They also do not take on everyone. Most likely your child will have to audition, even for their group classes. Your child will be expected to go to the coach every week for proper training.

If they think your child can succeed, they will accept them.

PILOT SEASON

If you have a really good coach, they will want you to take your child to New York, Vancouver, Atlanta or Los Angeles for "Pilot Season" when they feel your child is ready. If you go before your coach says your child is ready, you are wasting your money!

Pilot Season casting starts around March for the summer TV and film pilot shooting season. You have to consider carefully if your family can afford to go to either coast, find housing and stay for the entire casting season. Usually from March well into summer. There is also the gas to get back and forth from all the auditions.

If one parent goes, will there be proper supervision and nurturing for those siblings left at home.

When I was developing Margo Harshman (Tawny Dean on Disney's Even Stevens®), her mother drove 160,000 miles back and forth to auditions before Margo got the recurring role of Tawny Dean on Even Stevens® with Shia LaBeouf. Margo lived about 100 miles from Hollywood. The audition usually takes about 10 to 15 minutes. So, it meant driving 200 miles for a fifteen-minute audition.

Margo's grandmother moved into the house so the other three siblings would have proper care and attention.

Margo's mother put food, a compact port-o-potty and clothing changes in their minivan and Margo would do her homework on the way to and from the auditions. Margo also drove 200 miles to Hollywood once a week for her coaching classes.

When other children are playing with their friends, your child may be riding to auditions.

Very few child actors have been unscathed by the skewed values of the entertainment industry.

Something to think about the next time Granny tells you how cute your child is, and that you should get your child an agent.

THE SUBLIMINAL PARENT

34 BUILDING AN EXCELLENT CHILD

No matter what you tell your child, they learn from you SUBLIMINALLY.

If you smoke pot, no matter how surreptitious you think you are being, no matter how well you hide your stash, your child will know it. They will perceive it as acceptable ADULT behavior because YOU are their "Acceptable Adult"! You are subliminally training your child what is acceptable adult behavior.

If you abuse alcohol, your actions are telling your child that alcohol abuse is acceptable adult behavior.

If you physically abuse your child, you are teaching your child that physical abuse is acceptable adult behavior. It is not uncommon for children who are abused by adults to abuse siblings or schoolmates. They learned it from the parent, and they are passing it on. They equate this behavior as acceptable. Later it is common that they will abuse their own children. A sad Daisy Chain.

When your child is reaching out to establish their own adult identity, do not be surprised if they copy your behavior. No matter what you TELL them. This is, in many instances, the way they try to show you THEY are an adult. This is how they define their own "grown up" behavior.

Most important, your child will hear you, even when you don't think they are listening. The more you whisper, the harder they will listen! They will hear you verbalize what you believe. They will see how you treat others.

They will hear your prejudice, or your lack of it. They will hear you telling "white lies" to friends on the phone. When you instruct them to tell a caller you are not home, you are teaching them to lie. You are teaching them it is acceptable adult behavior to tell lies.

Everything you do and say is a teaching moment for your child! Remember they are learning from you subliminally!

Children are most open to learning from 0 to 5 years old. Before many parents realize how aware their children are, they have learned greatly from them. Then their learning curves level off and diminish over their lifetime. This is a child's most formative period.

You are building your child with your values subliminally.

Statues in parks do not make racists, expressed thoughts, actions, and shared beliefs make racists. By the same token, expressed thoughts and beliefs make world-class humans if the right thoughts are verbalized.

You, as your child's parent and primary mentor, must decide early on what you want to pass on to your child. You must decide what you may want to change about yourself and not pass on to your child.

Remember the old adage: "Little Teapots Have Big Ears!"

If you don't want your child to inherit some of your actions or prejudices, YOU NEED TO CHANGE YOUR BEHAVIOR WHEN AROUND YOUR CHILD.

Your child learns from your actions and words not only to them, but to others as well. They do not learn from what you tell them, to a child that is white noise. Make sure what you tell them is not different from your own actions. At all times remember your child is learning from both parents SUBLIMINALLY!

WHAT SHOULD I DO WHEN MY CHILD LIES?

Every parent knows when their child is telling a lie. Many times, the parent will choose to pretend not to know, to avoid an uncomfortable, or lengthy confrontation.

When your child lies, you need to hold them accountable **IMMEDIATELY**. You need to say without rancor, "I know that is not true, what is really going on? What is the truth?" Keep at it until your child tells you the real story. You will only need to do this a few times before they realize lies are fruitless. The minute you let your child get away with a lie, you have opened a door best left closed.

Teach your children early that you know when they try to

lie. Don't endorse their lie by pretending you don't know they are lying. Don't advocate lying by your avoidance of the issue.

Children learn quickly, they will either learn that they can get away with lies, or that they might as well tell the truth.

You need to get your child into the habit of telling the truth very early. If you don't, they will build up a habit of lying, assuming there will be no repercussion. This can impact them badly in adult life.

35 PARENT'S PUBERTY SURVIVAL GUIDE

Your child will survive puberty; this chapter will help the parent survive as well.

"Our house was a war zone. My children caused so much violence and chaos I was at the end of my rope. Now, after using Meredith Day's parenting methods, we all get along and I am so happy." *Lonnie B.*

First one must understand the evolution of puberty.

In the animal kingdom, when the young cub is old enough to be on their own, they will fight, and the mother will typically drive them off. It is no different with adolescent human children. Conflict is a naturally evolved way to cause the young adult to leave the nest.

From approximately 12 years old to as old as 25 an

individual suffers from significant brain chemistry changes. These changes outwardly show as conflict with the parents.

For no reason at all, the child will exhibit hate and intolerance for the parents. The same child who has been a loving companion up to this time.

In cave man days, this signaled that the young adult was ready to leave the parents and establish his own "tribe" identity.

This can be a frightening period of time for a parent. Even a child with no sensitivity to ADD triggers or Autistic Spectrum will go off the handle when an adolescent.

It's not uncommon for very well-adjusted children to feel at times worthless, powerless., enraged. The child flails about, lost in an unidentified rage one minute, loving and affectionate the next. They seem like a ticking bomb.

In 6th grade children seem to go through a brain drain. They forget everything they have been taught. They vacillate between wanting independence and taking their stuffed toys to bed.

They do homework and forget to turn it in. They forget assignments and test the convenient lie escape.

The only difference between a 6th grader and a 2 year-old is the size of their shoes due to the brain chemistry changes going on.

As the child progresses to 7th and 8th grade the insecurity gets worse. They feel impelled to taunt and deride those different from themselves in order to feel "bigger" themselves. They tear down others unmercifully in order to "elevate" their own self-esteem.

Anything can trigger the derision from clothing color to behavior to a physical handicap or hair color difference. One day they are the perpetrator, the next the recipient.

Even children, who are not sensitive to ADD triggers or Autistic will fidget, cough and belch in class and at home for effect. This is a natural rite of passage, NOT behavior requiring chemical intervention.

What is required at this time is extreme parental patience. Magically one day all the misbehavior will cease. Your child will revert to the respectful, well-behaved child he was prior to his pubescent evolution.

In order to nurture your child, you must draw a very large circle of love around him. Give him space to "collect his thoughts" when you would rather make wall decor out of him.

Put your hands deep in your pockets when your child dishes out extremely rude verbal abuse. Parents have to learn to take very deep breaths, and not return the anger that appears to be directed at them. When they are being rude and abusive remove yourself from their presence. Let them be isolated with their angst.

Adolescent anger is merely an unfortunate, predictable side effect of the puberty process, similar to the "terrible 2s'. It is indicative of the child striking out to find his own individuality, trying to find his self-worth. Trying to prove he is an adult.

THE SUBLIMINAL PARENT

The parent needs to take a step backward and give the child the freedom to step away and cool off, rather than engaging in all out verbal war with the child. Remember violence returned generally escalates.

Just like the terrible twos, the parent is best advised not to return the level of anger. This is a crucial learning period for the child. Parental behavior under these circumstances becomes the "acceptable adult behavior" for the mature child. Do not reinforce the verbal abuse with verbal abuse. Calm the child by rational response, even if you have to break dishes in the garage later in private to release the parental tension.

Commonly runaway children fit into this age bracket. It is not unusual for the child to leave because the parent is returning the anger and potential violence in kind. This causes the child, not realizing what is going on in his own head, to want to strike out on their own. Just as it did in cave man days. Remember, that was the whole original design and purpose of puberty.

Child/Parent puberic verbal wars account for many homeless children living on the streets of large cities. The momentary rage is so powerful that the parent can mistakenly feed off it, delivering rage and ultimatums impossible to uphold with a confused transitioning adolescent child. Worse yet, this can lead to physical violence on one side or the other that you can never push the rewind button on.

For a child already sensitive to such things as ADD trigger chemicals or Autistic Spectrum, puberty is an extreme gauntlet to cross. Not only do they have the same feelings of a normal developing adolescent, they are also intensely heightened by their spectrum. What might be simple rage in a normal child may become hopeless suicidal tendencies in sensitives.

The parent must stay in tune with their child. If he expresses suicidal tendencies, IMMEDIATELY get the child psychological help as well as testing for all spectrum sensitivities. You child's life might hang in the balance.

The best cure is to forgive and to hug. A forgiven child can bounce back. A hug, when the child will accept it, reinforces the closeness that they still need. They won't have to search for the love and reassurance they really want from the parent through gangs, drugs, alcohol or promiscuous sexual behavior.

Saving the best for last, I have to relay the advice of a parent who raised four sons successfully.

When my own son hit 12 and did a major Dr. Jekyll/Mr. Hyde on me, I called her and asked for advice.

Here it is:

When your child is going crazy and storms into his room slamming the door, DON'T FOLLOW THEM IN!

If you leave them alone, they will cool down, and come out in a while and tell you what really happened that day that set them off.

If you follow them in, ("Don't you slam the door on me!") you are just guaranteeing that world war three will escalate and go for hours. In many cases end VERY badly.

The next time it happened with my son, I didn't follow him in. I sat immobile on the couch nauseous. It was all I could do to control my own anger.

Eventually my son came out and tearfully told me what had happened at school that had put him in the rage.

If your own children are not getting along, give them their own space. If you have two children in puberty in your household and they fight at breakfast, let them each have their own dining space. Say you have a son and a daughter that can't be in the same room without fighting. Let your daughter have her own "tea" area in her room with a small cafe table and chair. Let your son eat in the kitchen, both in peace. This way they don't go to school already in flight or fight adrenalin rush.

A big thank you to my friend, Ann Schulz, for giving me the advice that saved my relationship with my son. I hope I can do the same for you!

36 YOUR CHILD'S BRAIN

The most important muscle that needs exercise in your child's body is their brain. Their brain develops the fastest between birth and 5 years old. The parent's responsibility is to feed it well during that time.

The more varied the stimulation, both visual and audio, that you provide for your child during that time, the more of their brain synapses can connect and the bigger potential for high intelligence will be created.

Most parents are not aware that even when an infant, your child is taking in everything around them. This allows their brain to grow. Vary the surrounding even in their bedroom. Change the pictures on the wall. Leave Sesame Street on in the background.

Take your child on sightseeing trips to the Zoo, construction sites, anything that can trigger their brain development. Talk to you child even though you don't think they can understand you yet. When your child makes unintelligible sounds make sure to listen. In their brain they are expressing ideas even though you can't yet understand their words.

37 HOW TO FIGHT CHILDHOOD OBESITY

As I write this book there is a cultural acceptance of childhood obesity. Partly because our eating habits are so skewed from past generations.

In the past, great quantities of food were necessary because we were a much more active society. We burned off much more energy and needed large amounts of calories. Now we don't.

Currently, in first world countries, we are a basically sedentary society. We sit at desks; we sit in front of computer monitors and video games. We play with cell phones instead of sports. Because of this, our food/caloric intake has to be modified. We only need a fraction of the calories to run our car.

Many children that suffer from obesity live in families where everyone in the family is overweight. They learn their eating habits from their parents and long before they are making their own nutrition decisions, bad decisions are being made for them by their parents.

As a new parent, you must make a decision about how you are going to manage your child's health. You must put away, or not buy, the food with empty calories. You must remember that YOU are driving your child's car. Whatever he becomes as a child, you are responsible for. You are the artist of your child's development.

Early you must decide how you want to build your child: and do that.

38 LAST, BUT NOT LEAST

The most important thing you need to remember when making parenting decisions is:

You are in control of creating the child you want to have.

Whatever you tell your child they are, they will become.

If you tell your child they are kind and generous they will become that.

If you tell your child they are a bad kid, that is what they will strive to be.

They will do their best to be what you say they are. Your child wants to live up to your expectation of them.

Even if your child is really acting up and driving you crazy, tell them how great they are and what a good boy or girl for

_____ (fill in the blank here, pick something they did right).

You are all powerful, what you tell your child they are, is what they will become.

Your child will treat you with the same love, attention and respect that you show them.

Or very simply...

What you give is what you get.

ABOUT THE AUTHOR

Meredith M. Day is a true renaissance woman. Day was raised by an Architect/Structural Designer/Ecologist father, her mother, one of the first female Rocket Scientists and her Great Aunt, Ohio's esteemed educator Mary E. Case. Meredith was taught to believe "You Can Do Anything You Put Your Mind To" by her Great Aunt.

Day is a 3xs patented inventor and considered a pioneer in 3D photography and film. She has spent her life as: (in order of appearance) an actress, singer/songwriter, set designer, photographer, filmmaker, inventor, author, music producer, teacher and, for the last three decades, a talent scout – talent developer & manager.

Day founded "Mothers Against Child Endangerment" in 1992. Of all her endeavors, Day values highest her time as a child celebrity talent developer and mother. "Helping other parents with what I have learned along the way is a great way to give back."

Day has worked with celebrities such as Shia LaBeouf (Even Stevens, Transformers), Michael Jackson, James Brown, DiDi Benami (American Idol), Award Nominated, young autistic singer and voice talent Autumn Sky Wolfe (CdBaby - iTunes - Spotify - AMDA) Jason Castro (American Idol), Joe Walsh (The Eagles), Michael Welch (Star Trek/Twilight), Margo Harshman (Even Stevens/NCIS), Adrianne (AKA Adrianna) Leon (General Hospital/The Young and the Restless).

www.ingramcontent.com/pod-product-compliance
Lightning Source LLC
Chambersburg PA
CBHW071004080526
44587CB00015B/2341